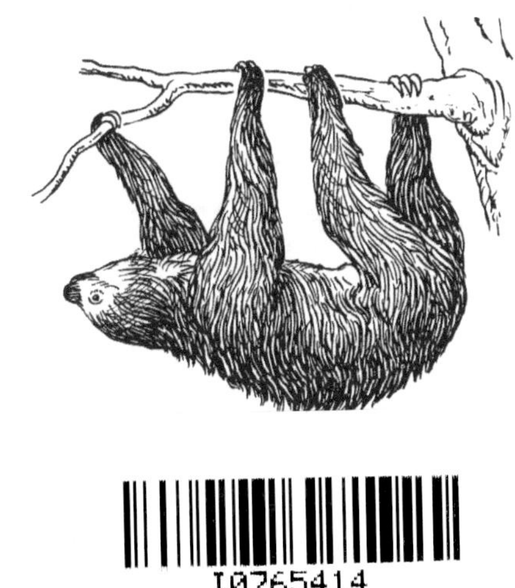

This Book Belongs to:

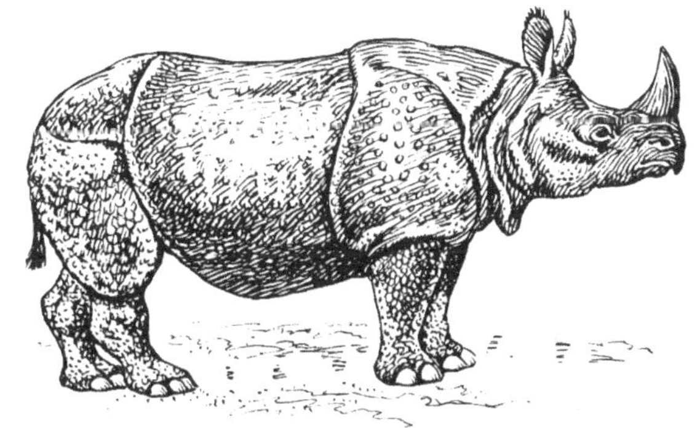

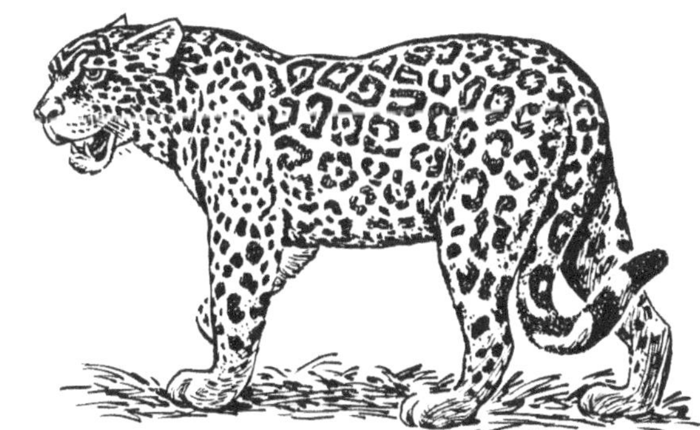

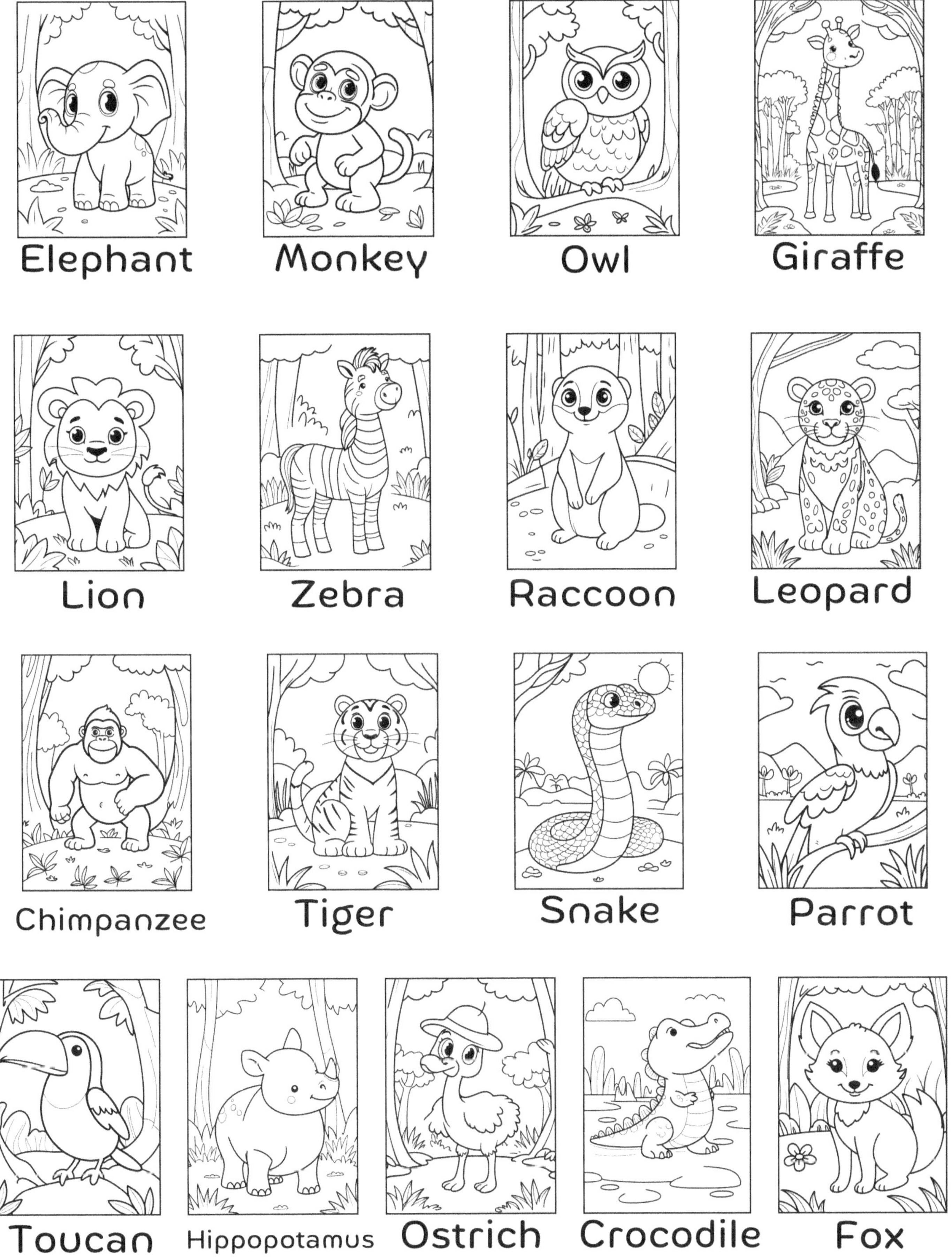

Elephant
Monkey
Owl
Giraffe
Lion
Zebra
Raccoon
Leopard
Chimpanzee
Tiger
Snake
Parrot
Toucan
Hippopotamus
Ostrich
Crocodile
Fox

Test Color Page

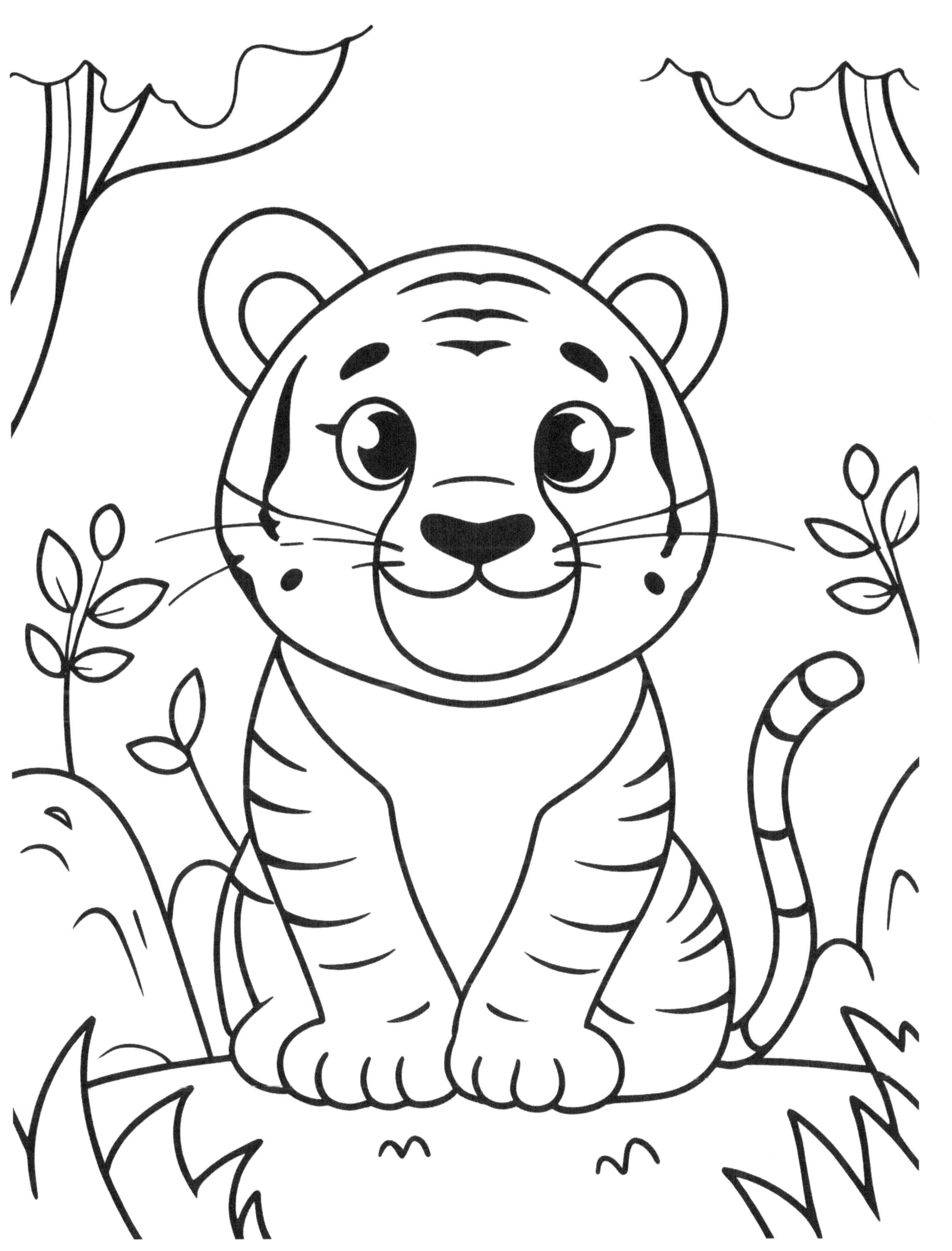

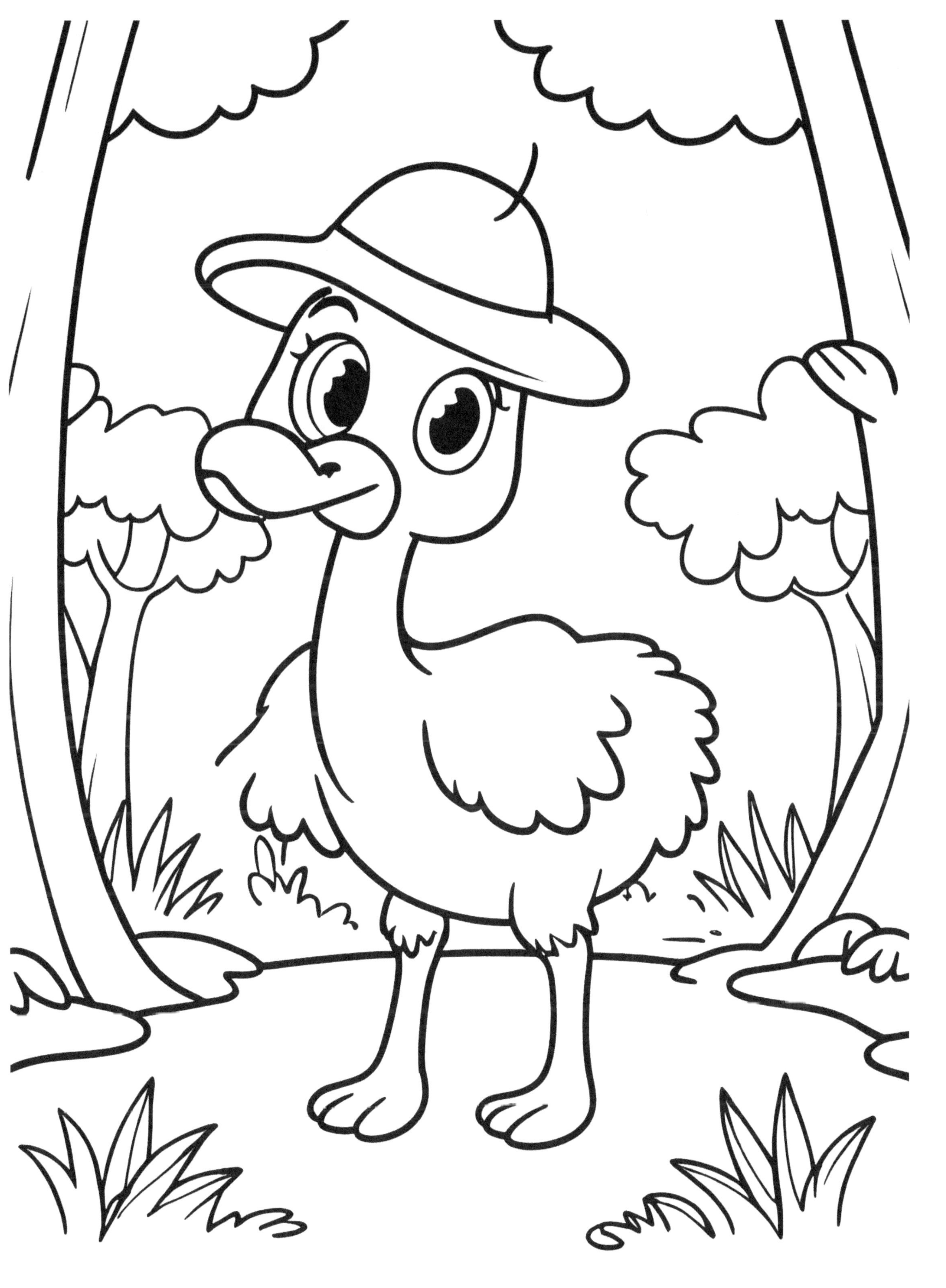

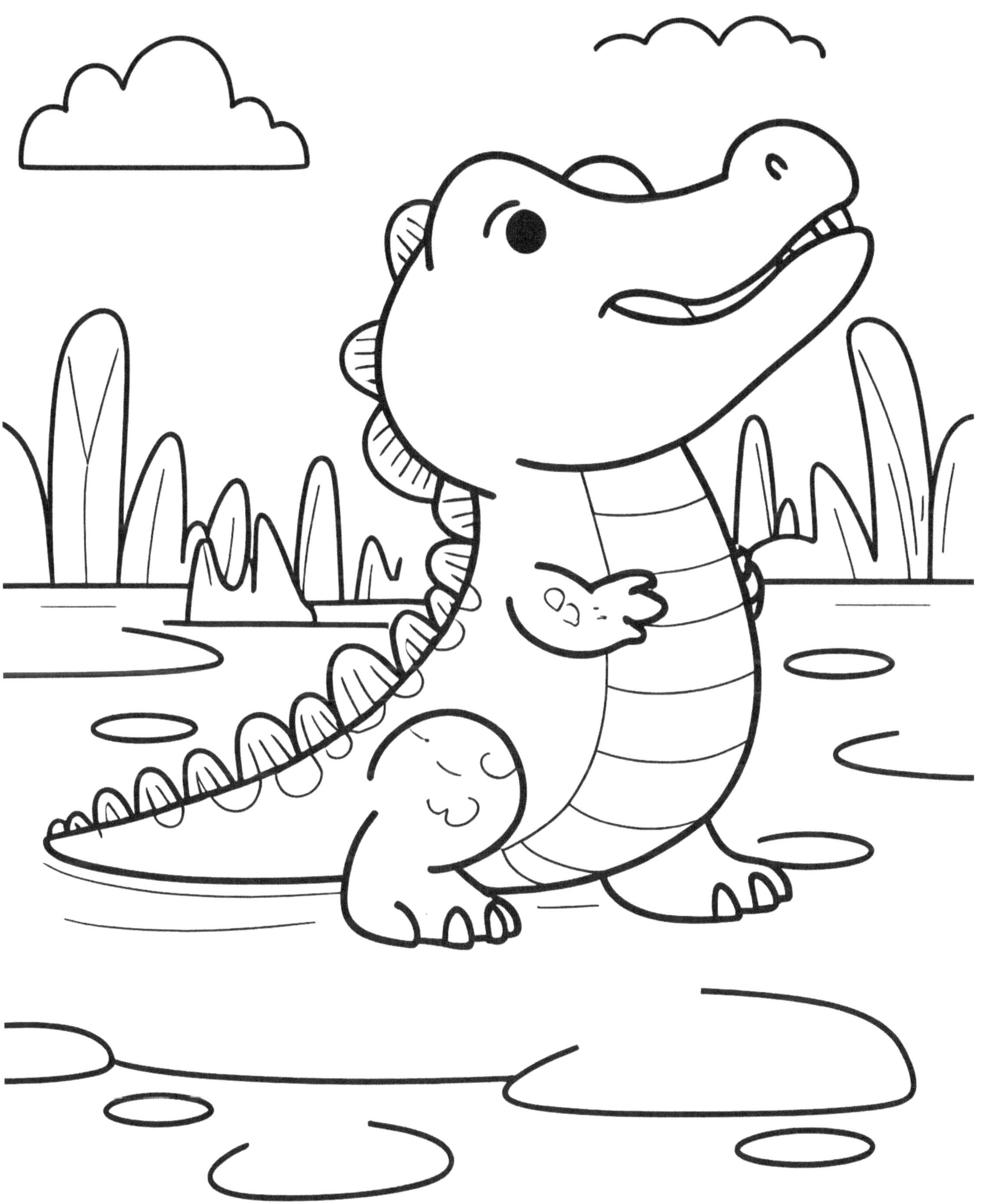

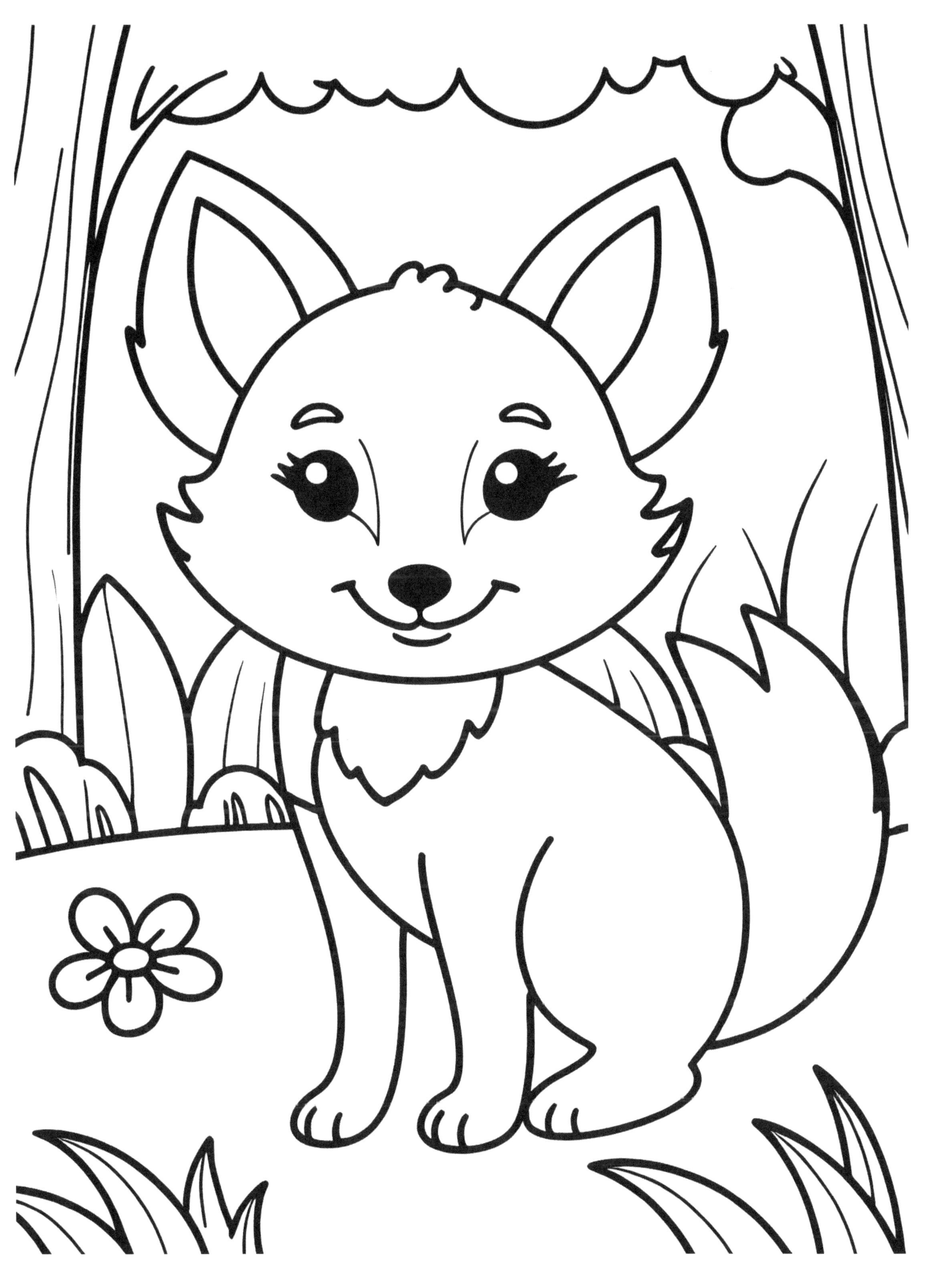

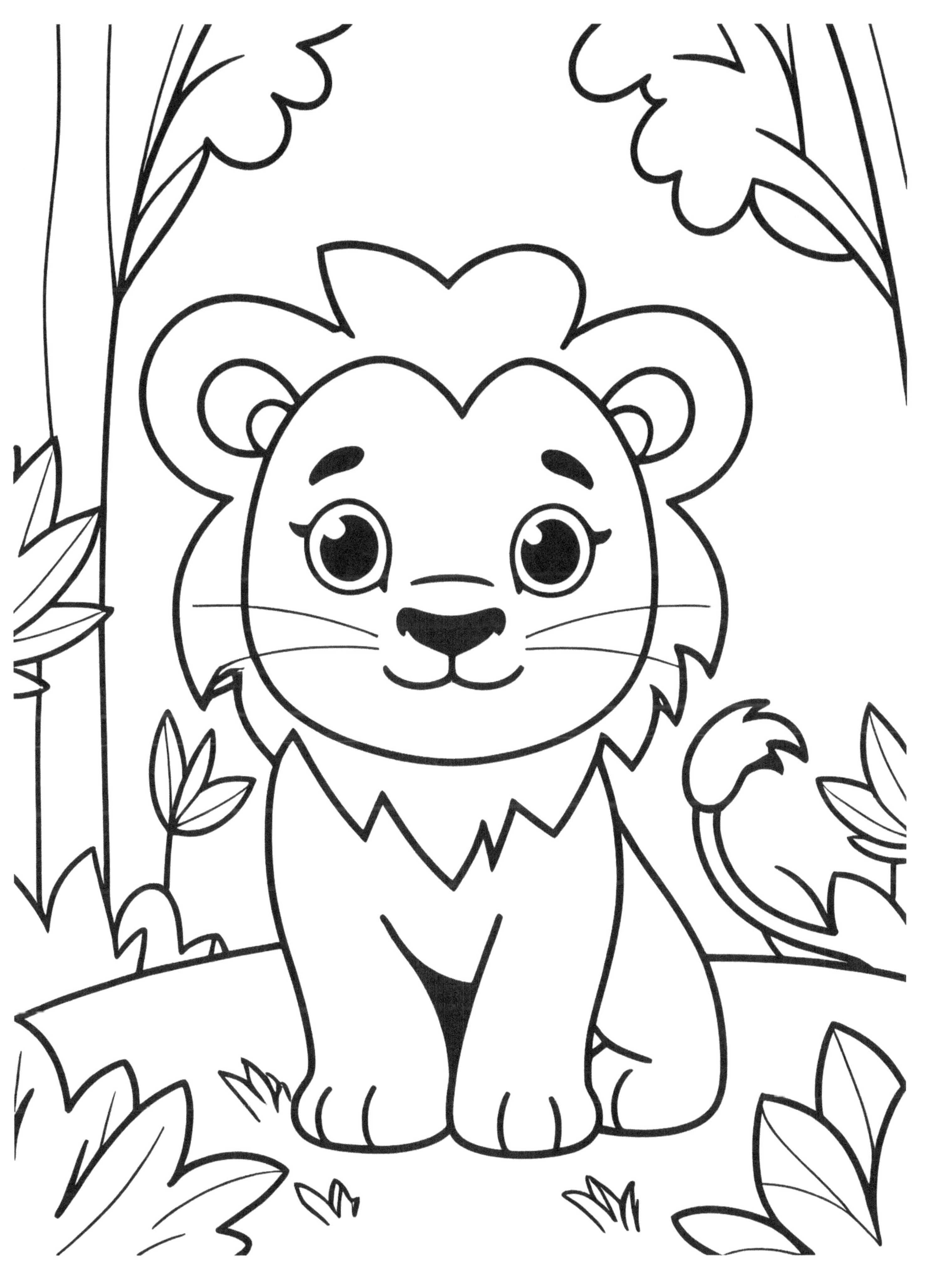

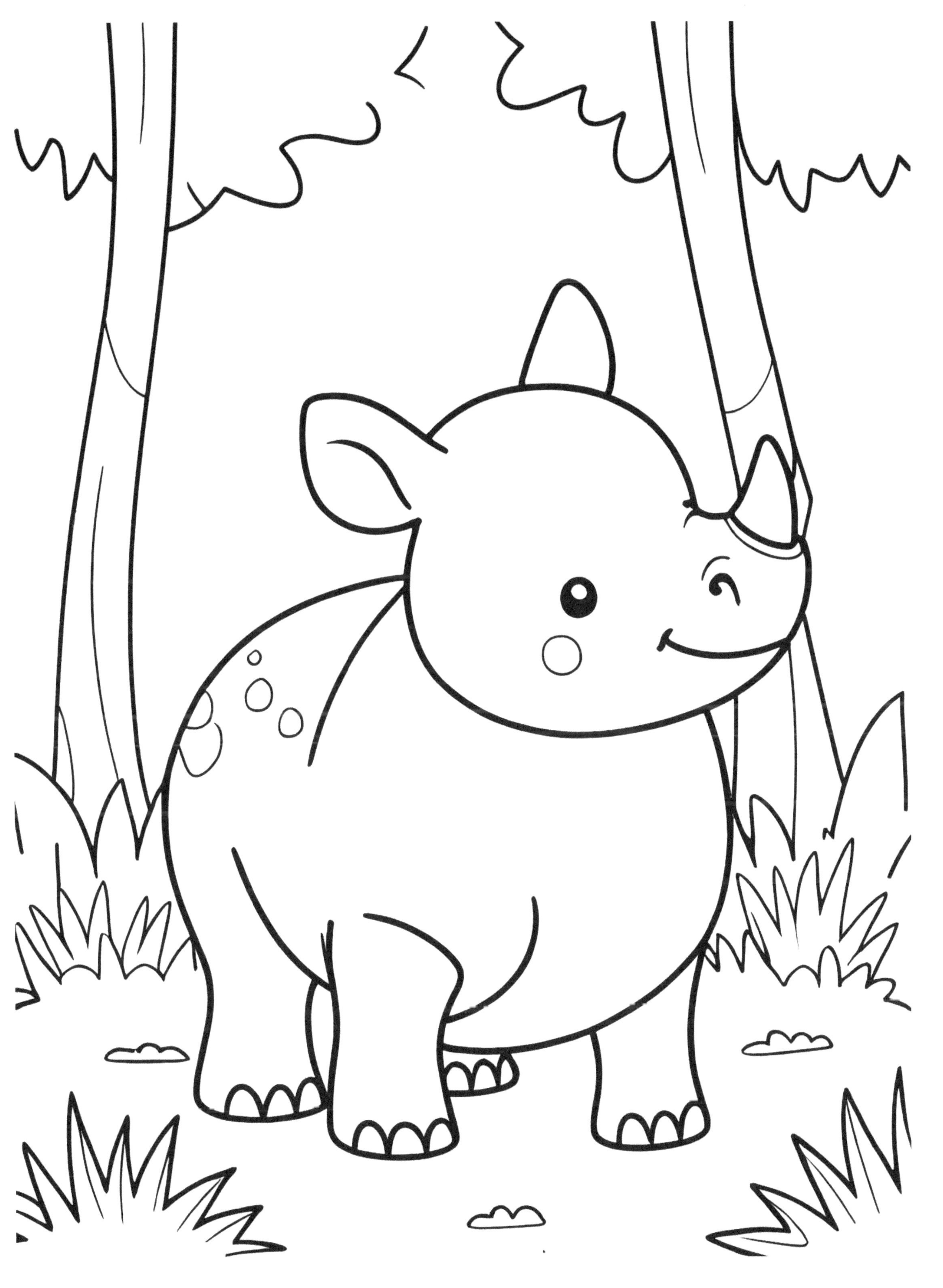

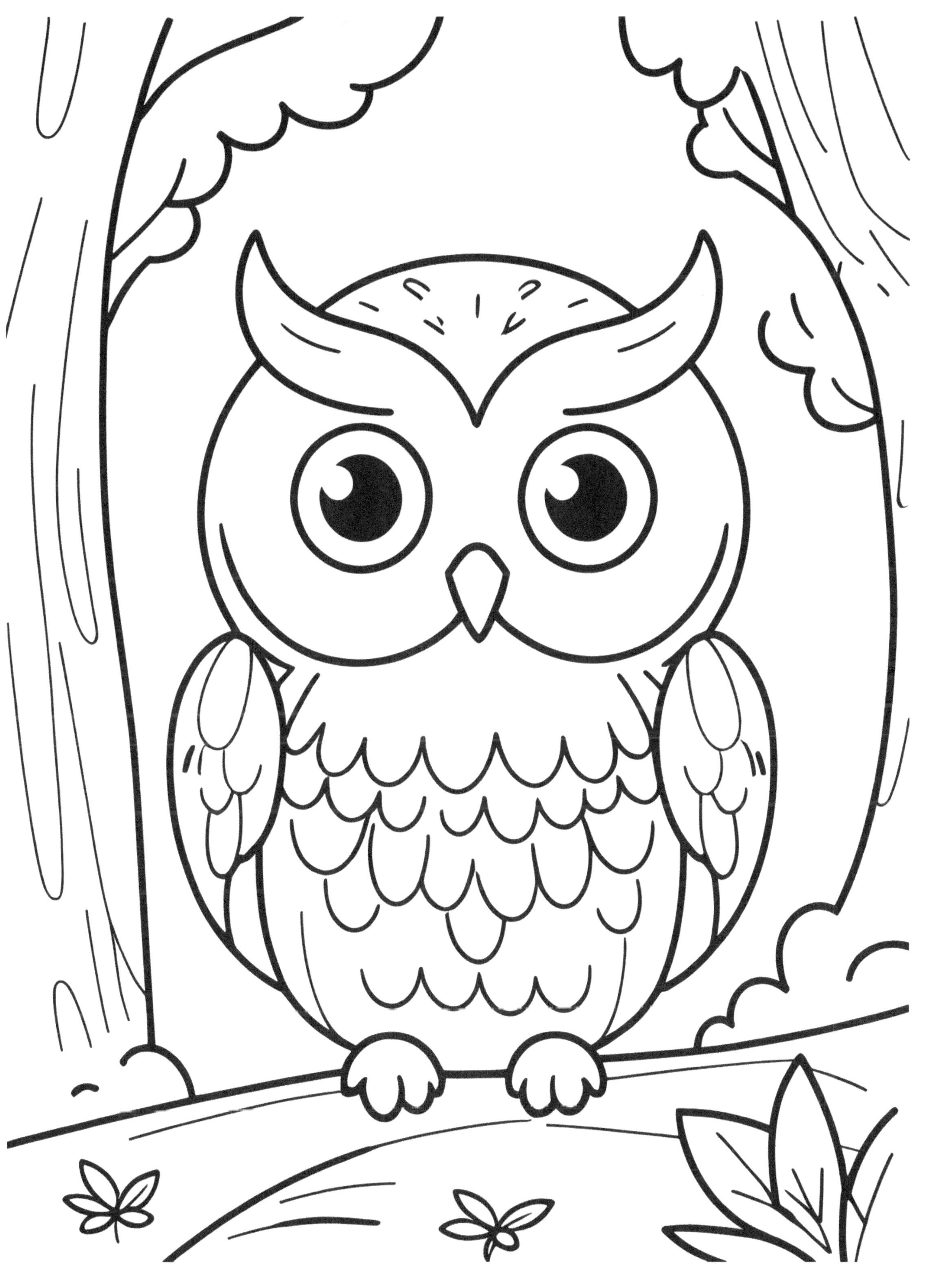

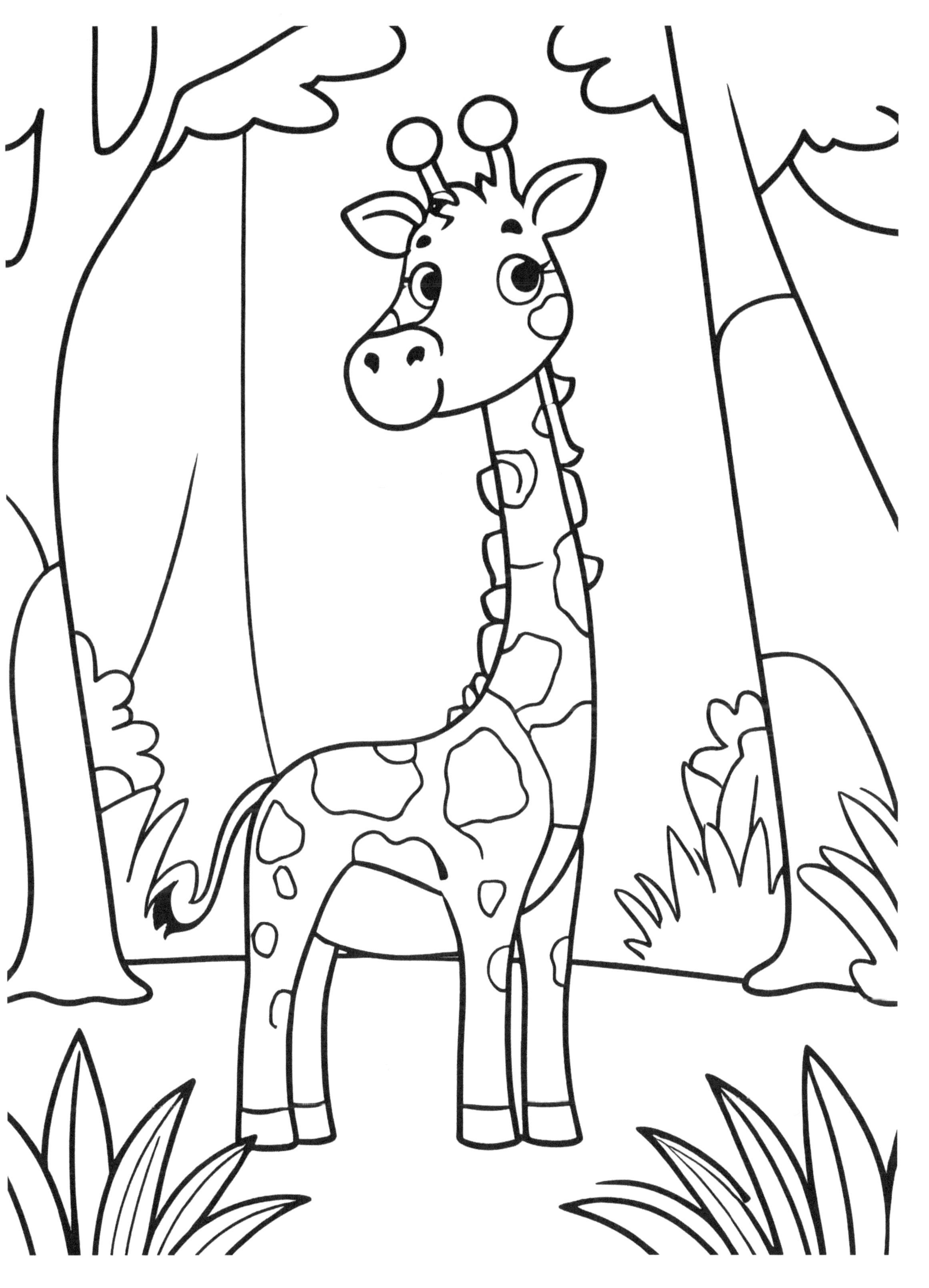

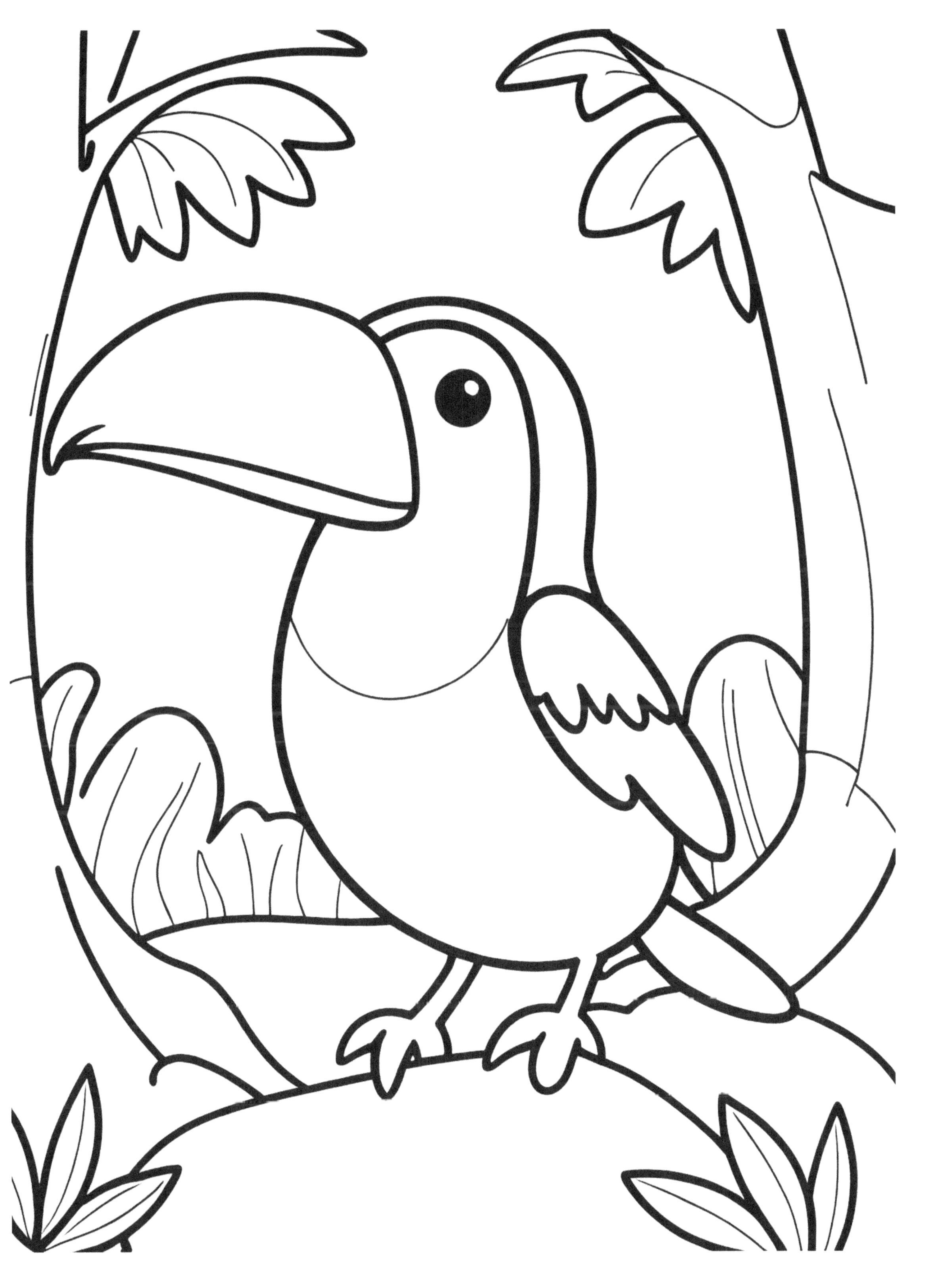

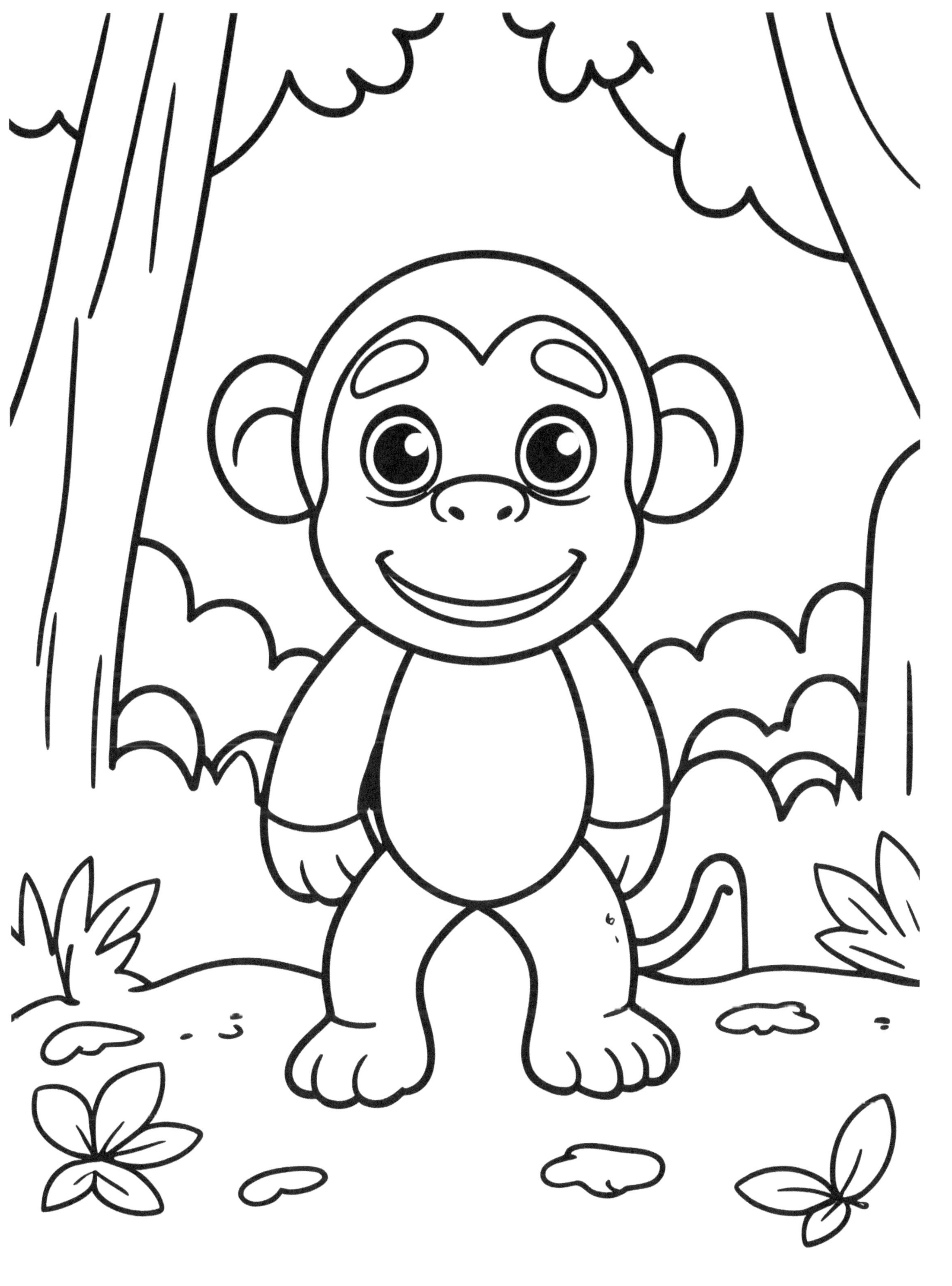

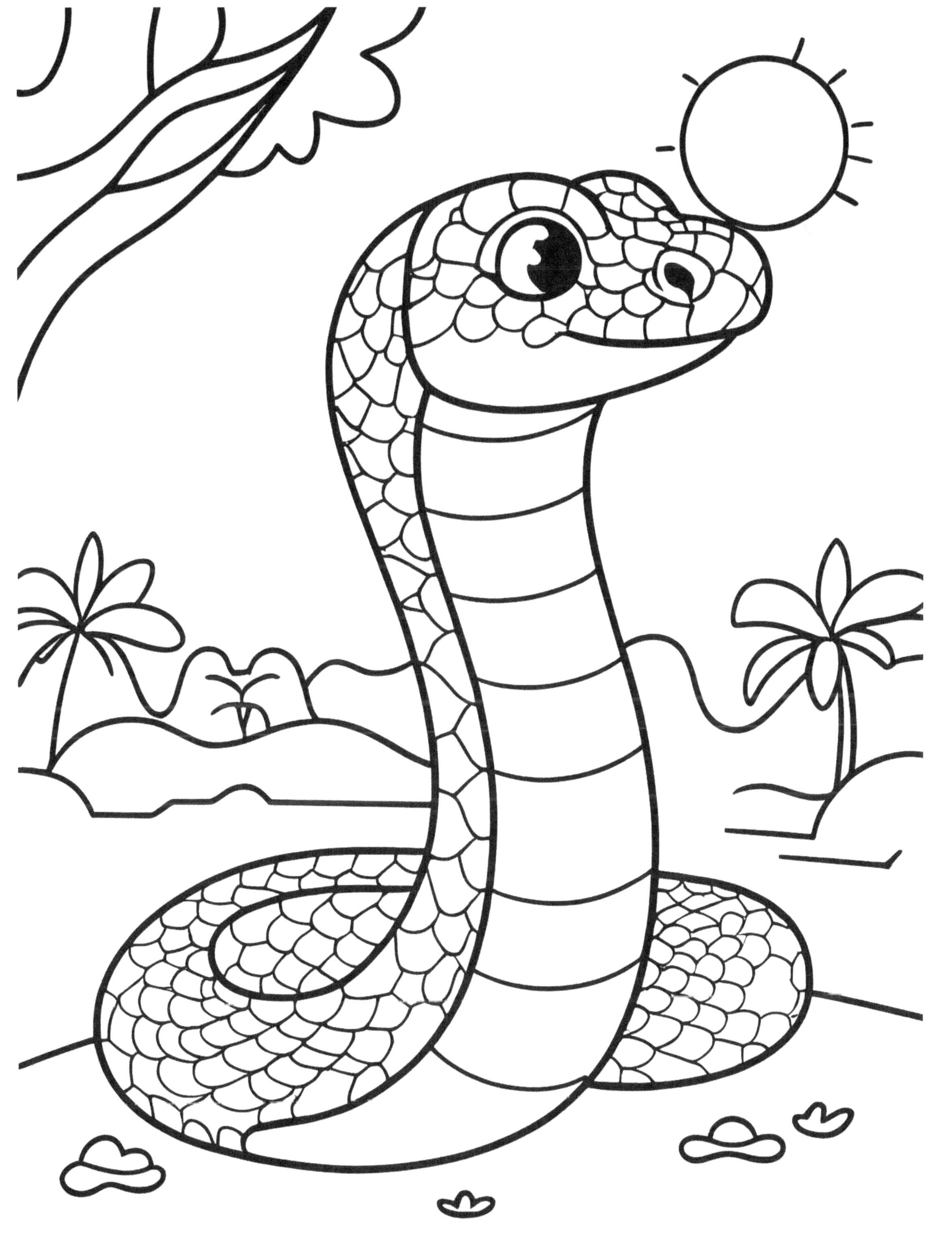

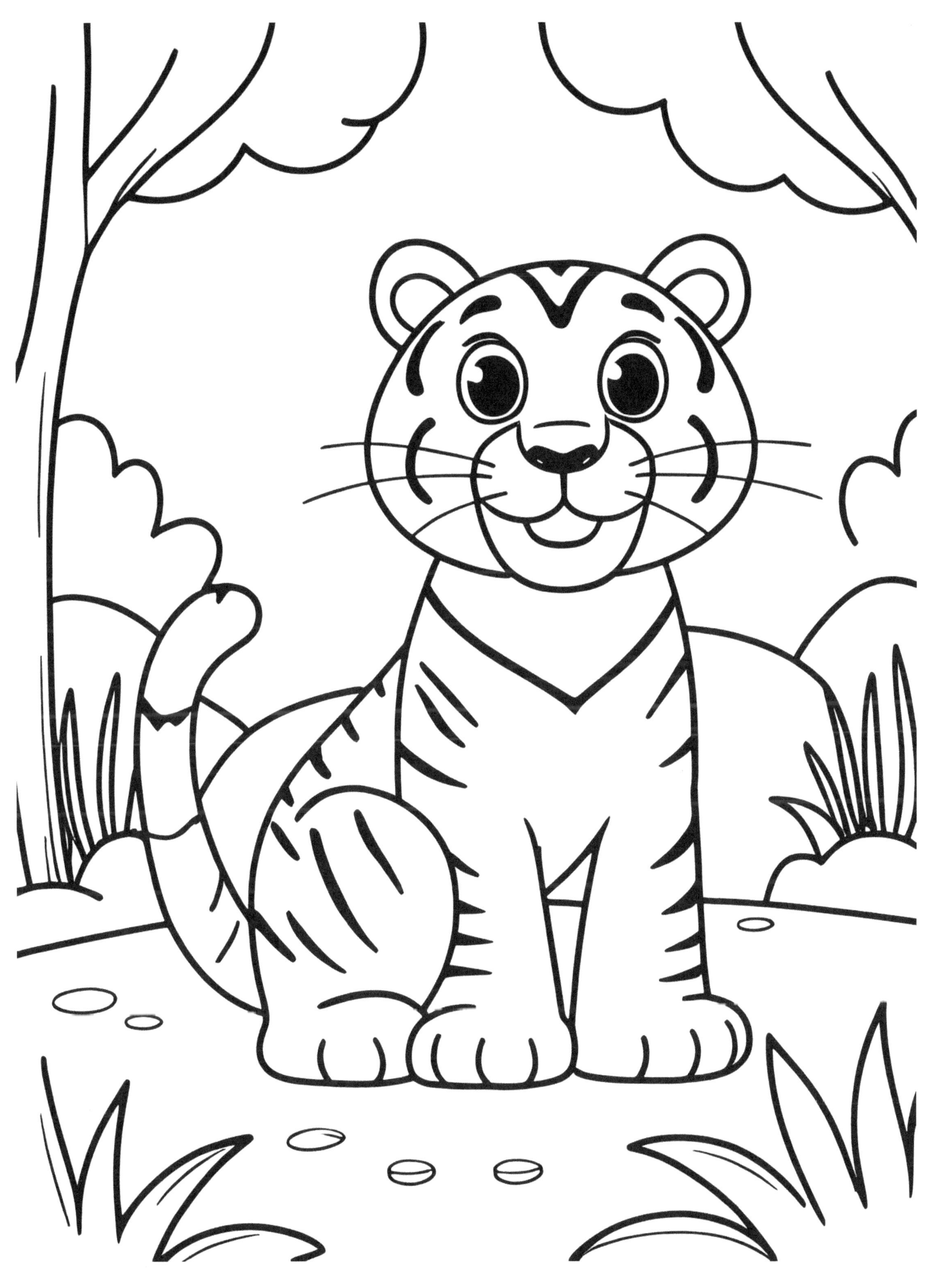

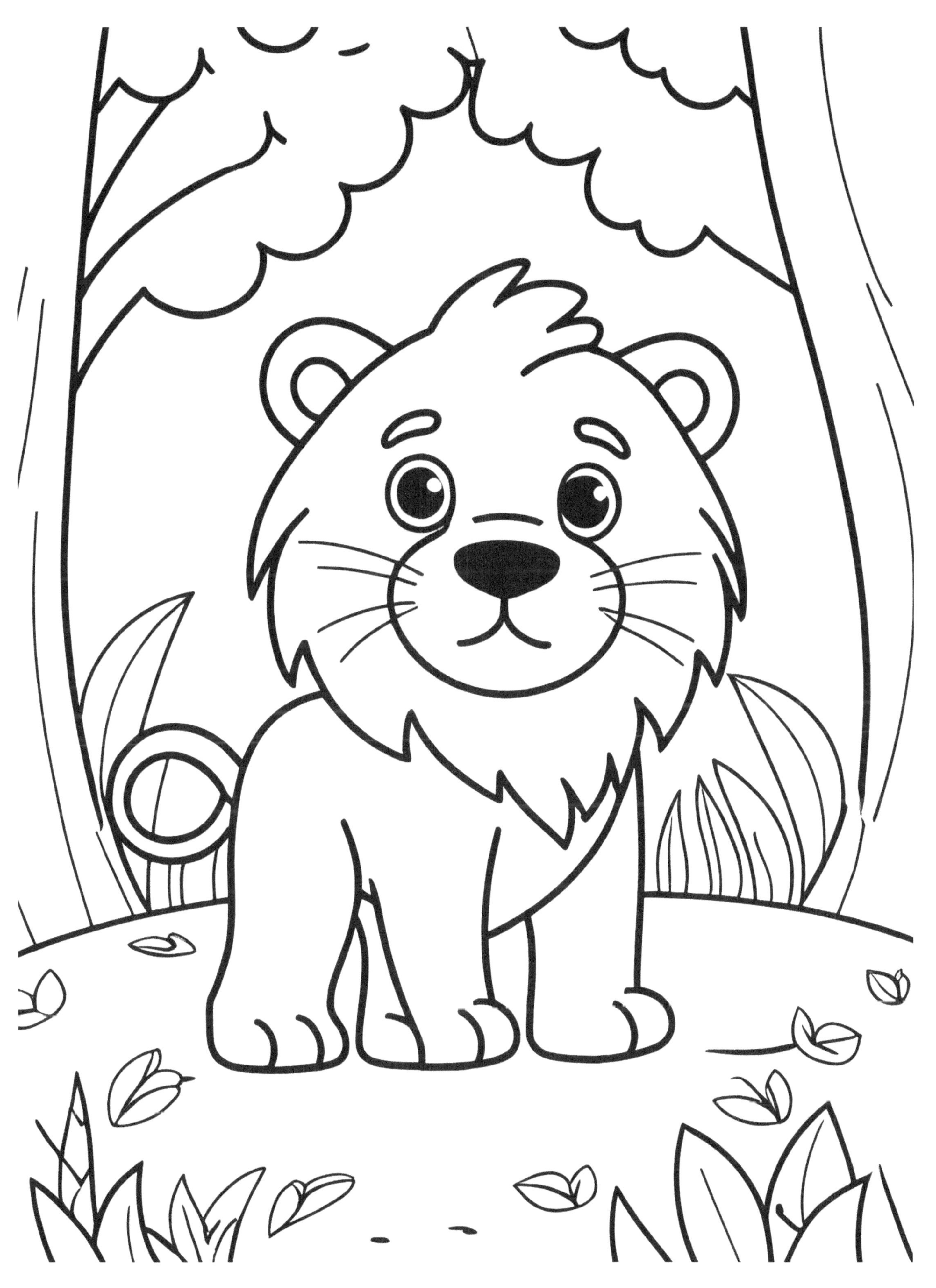

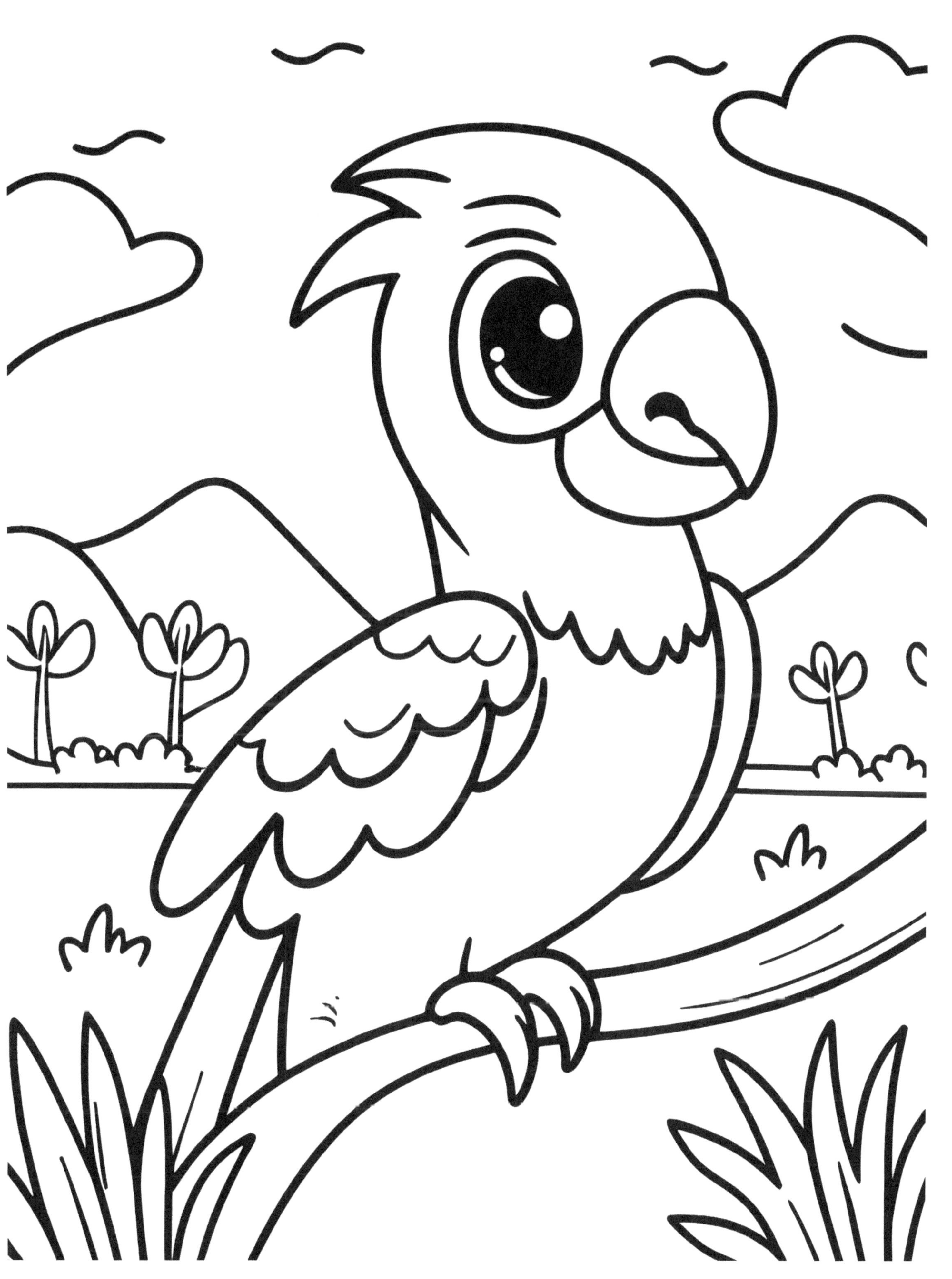

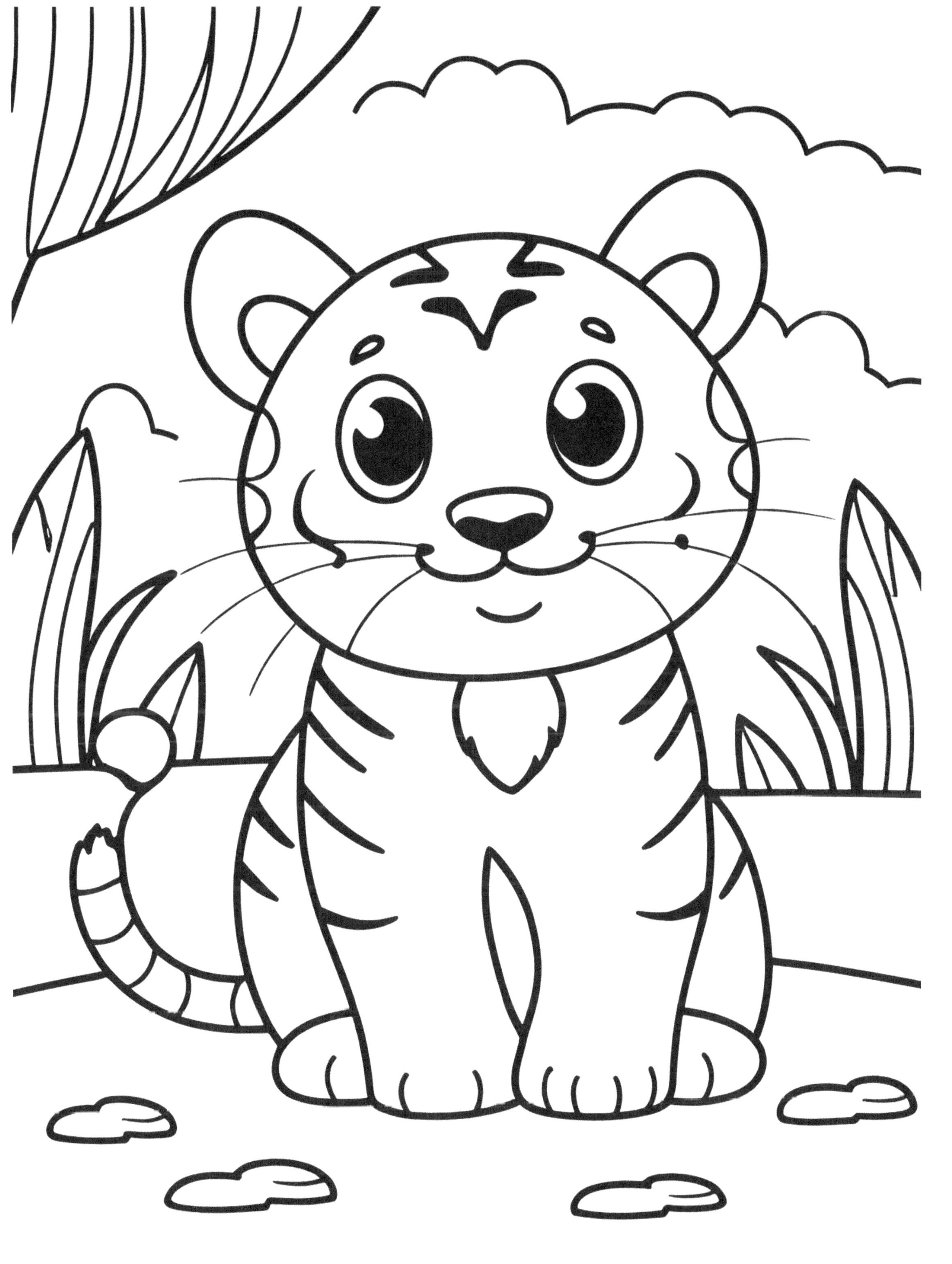

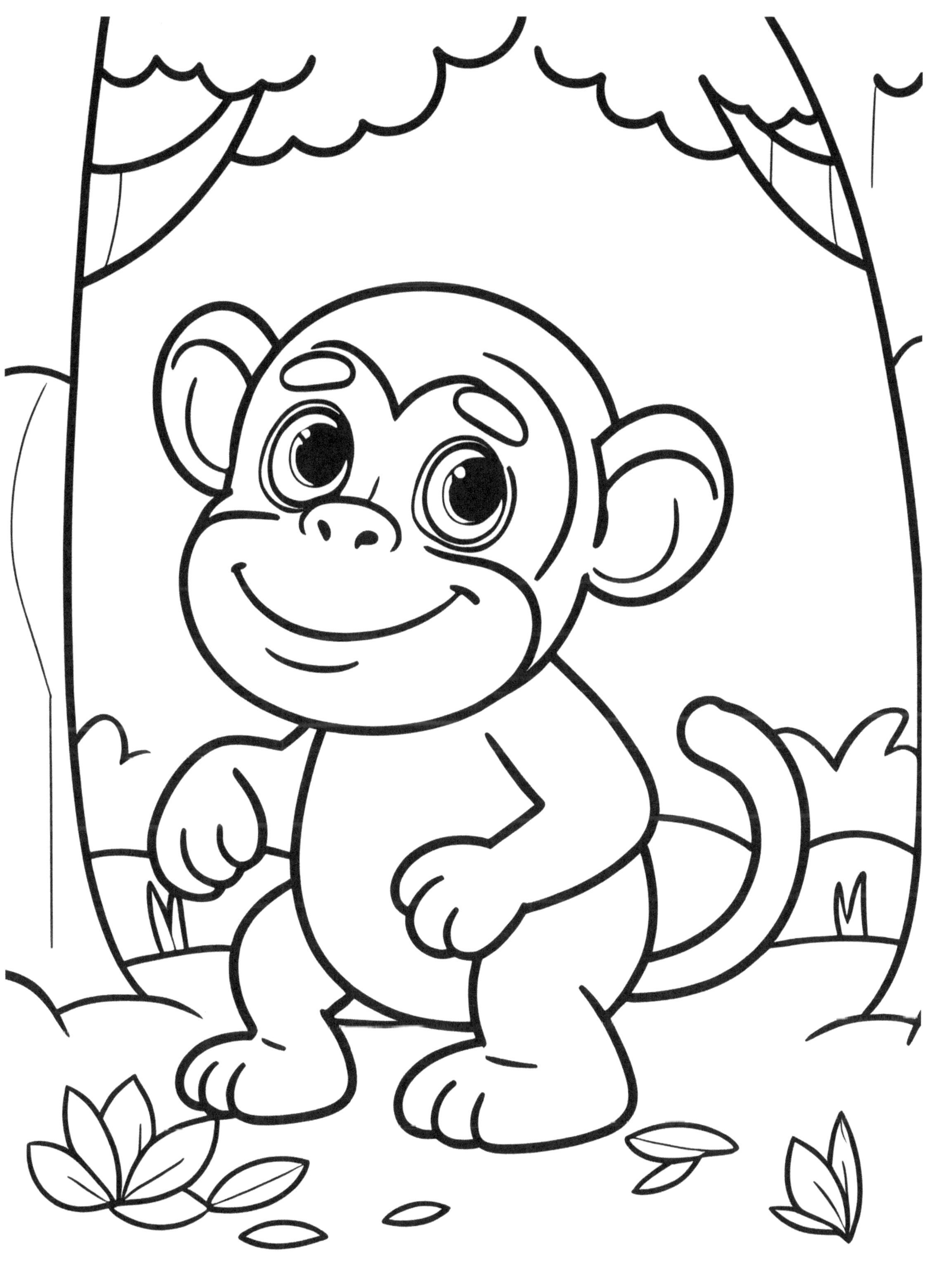

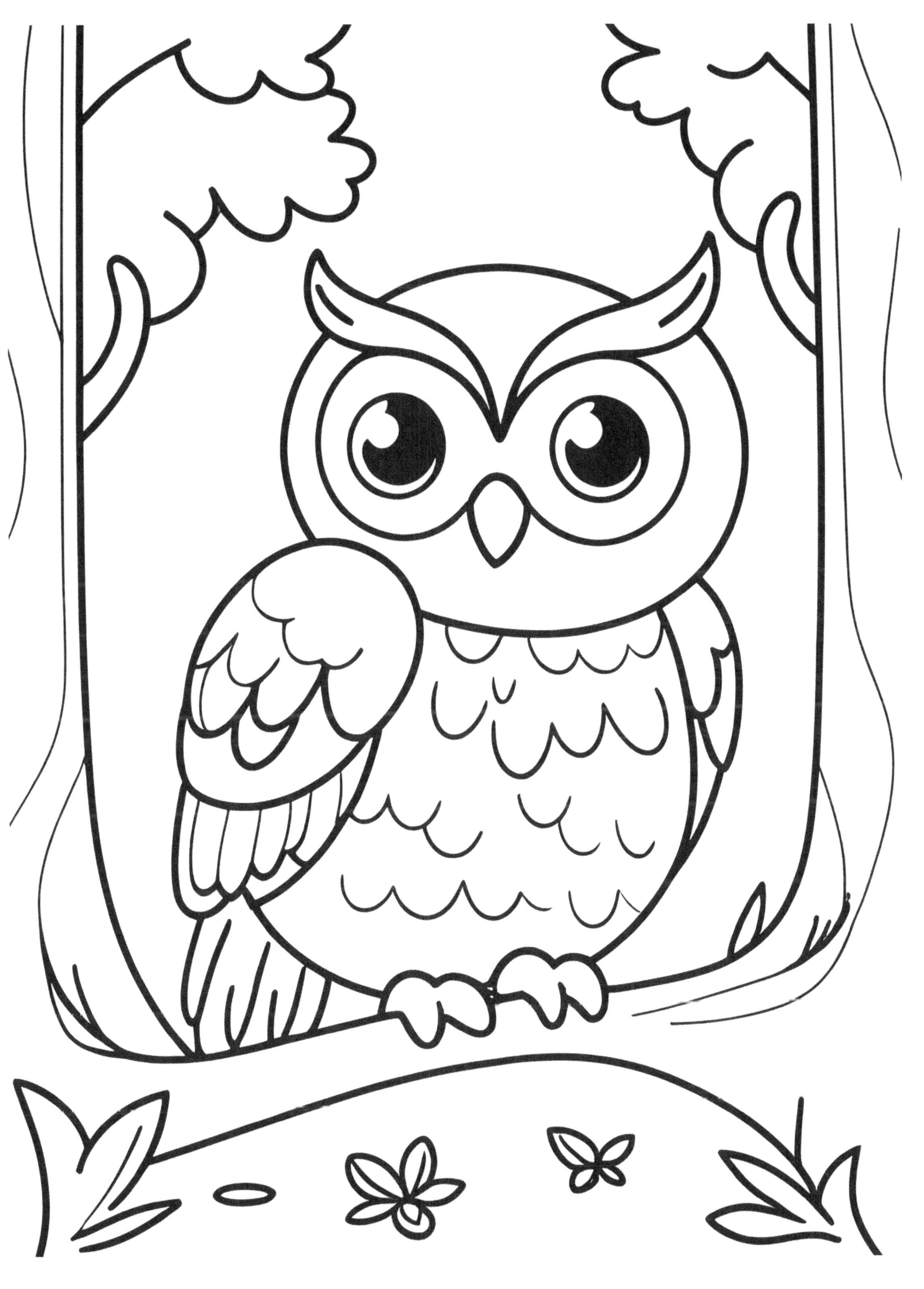

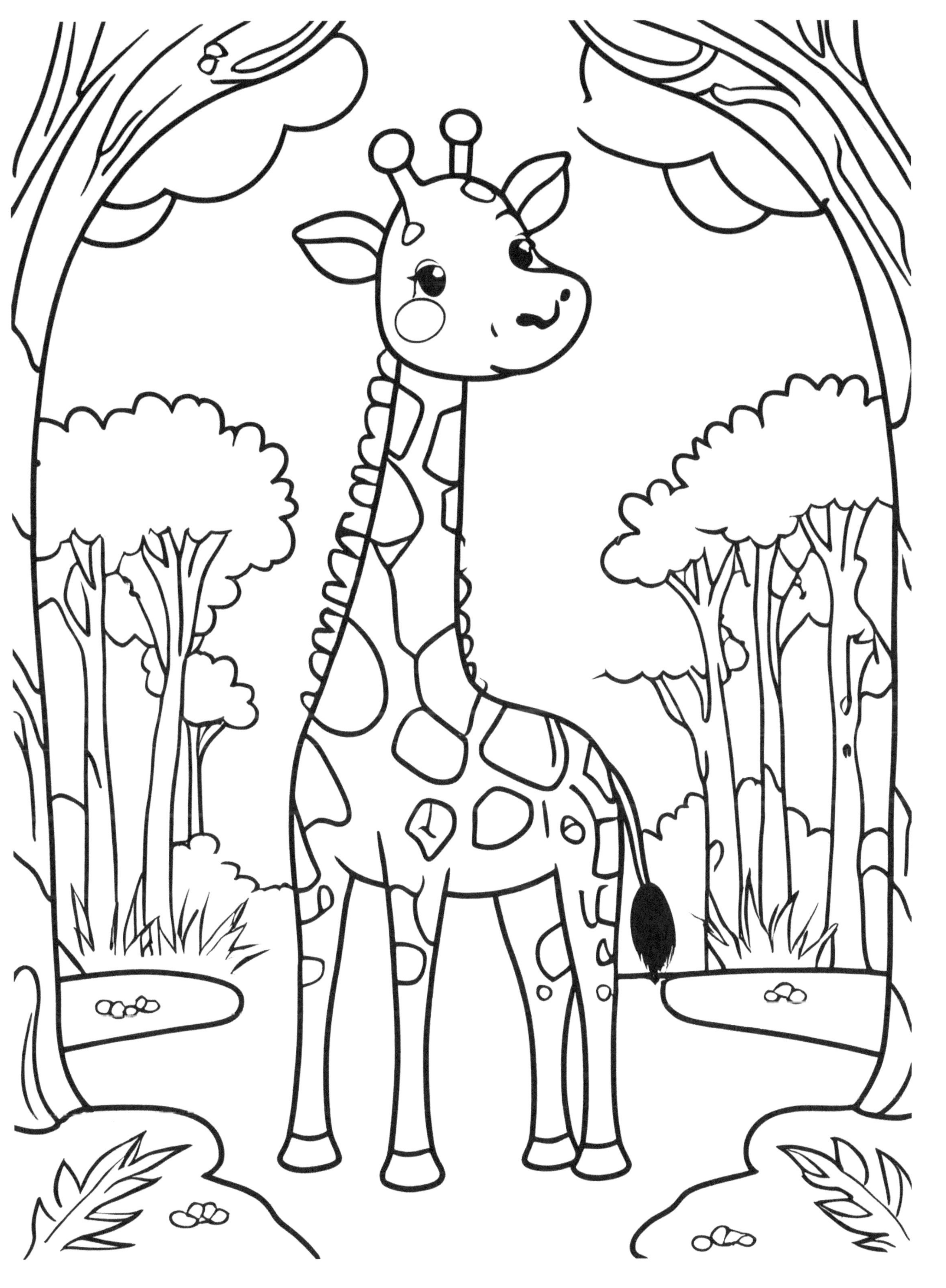

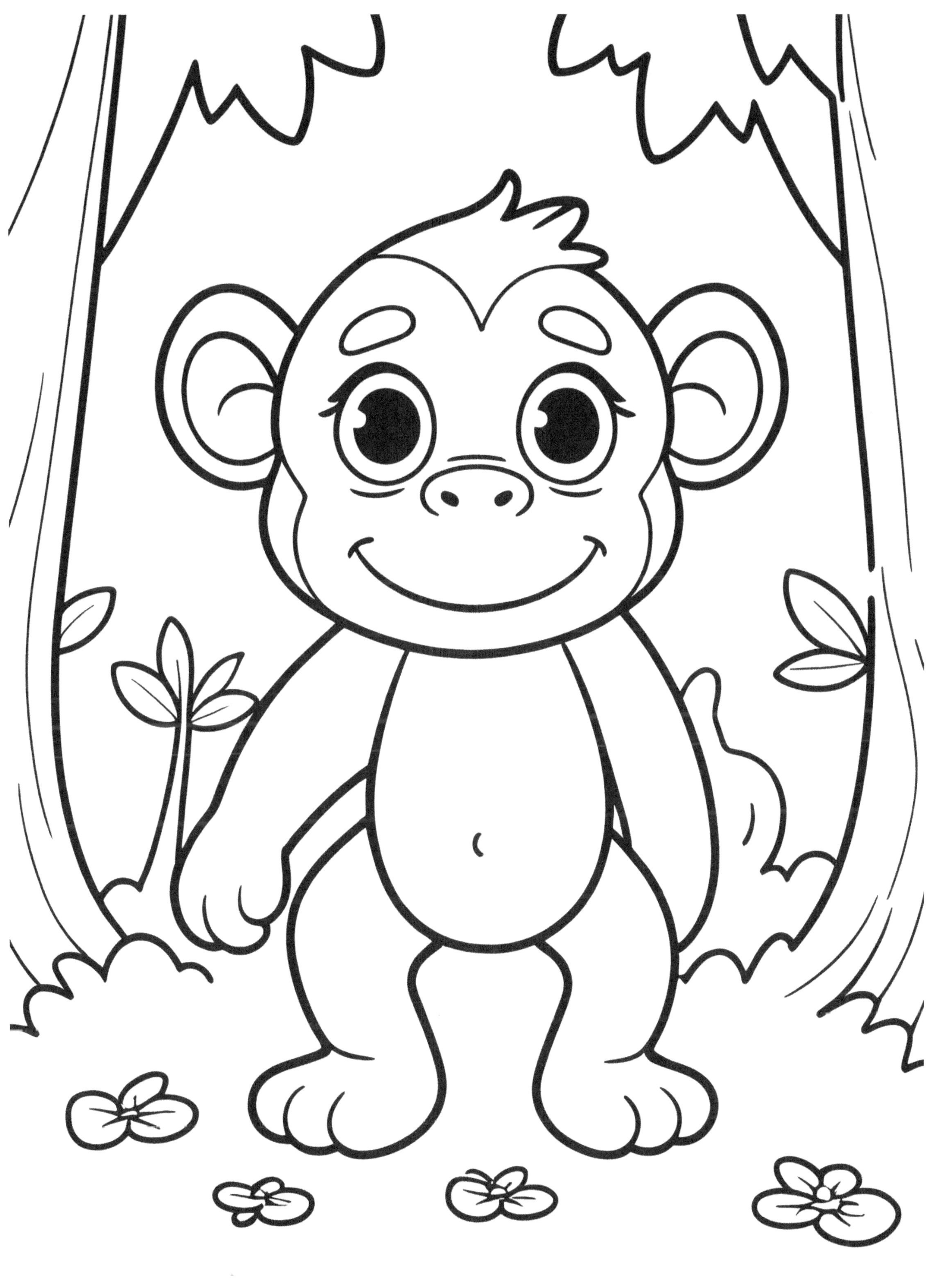

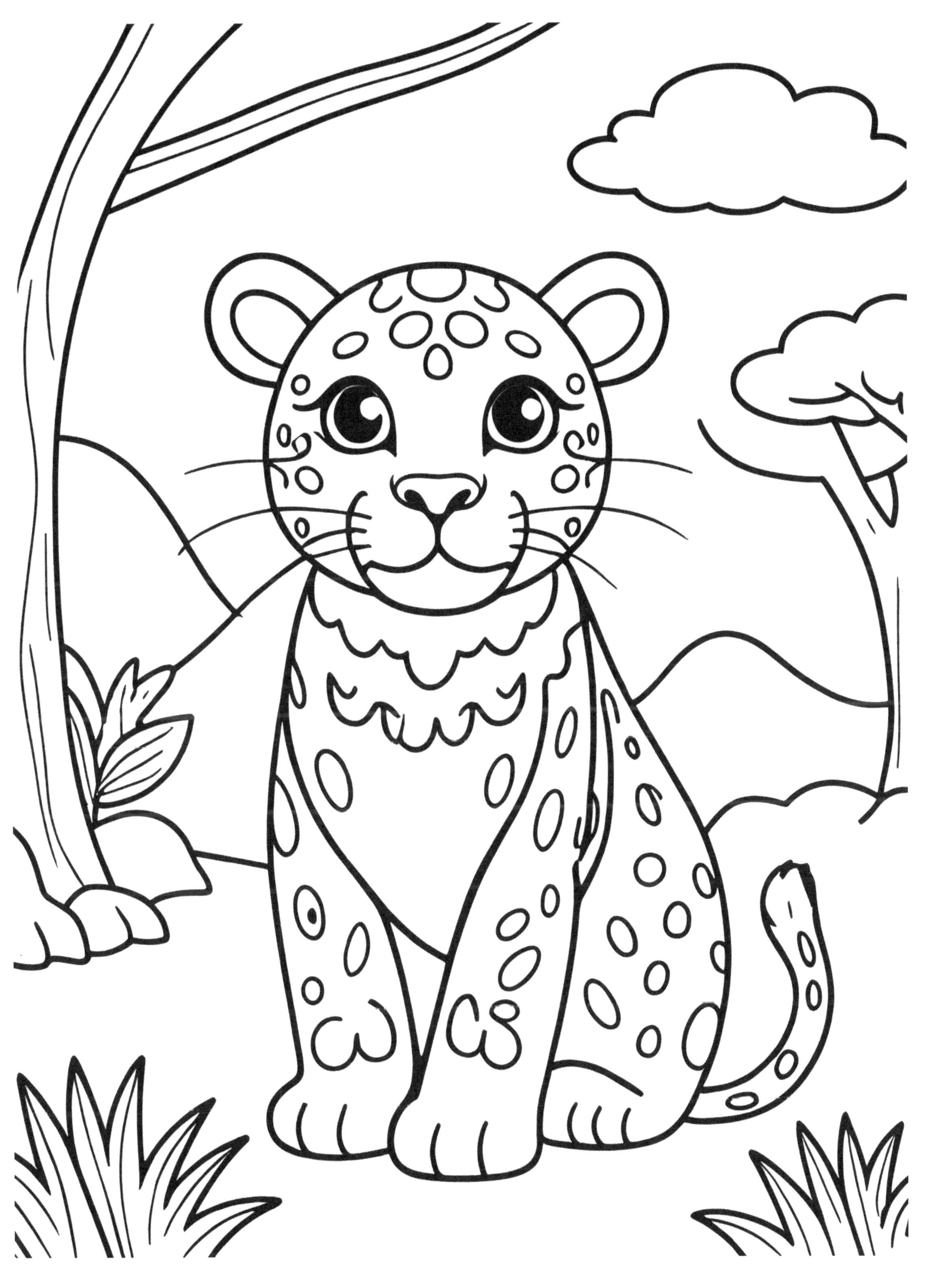

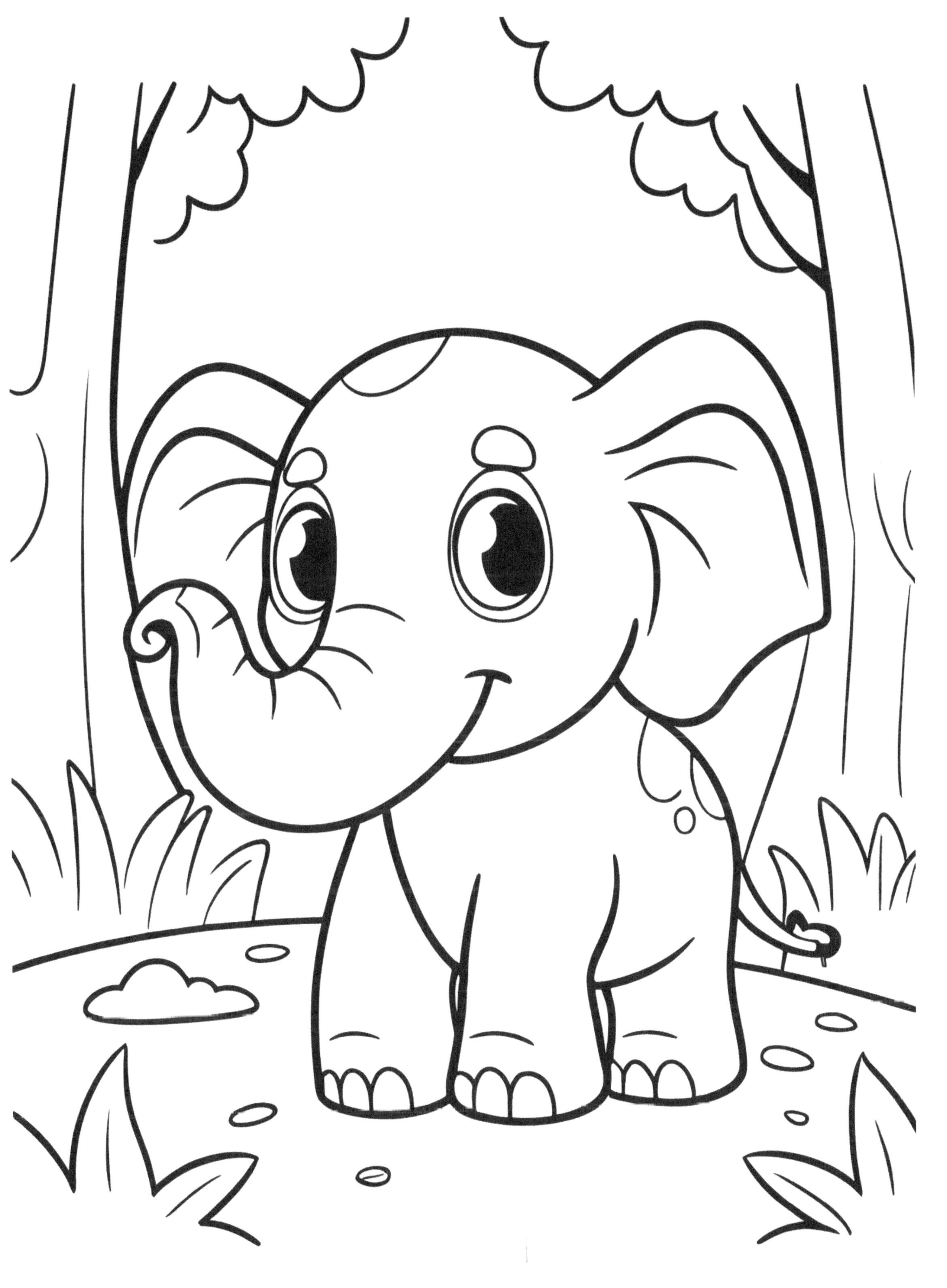

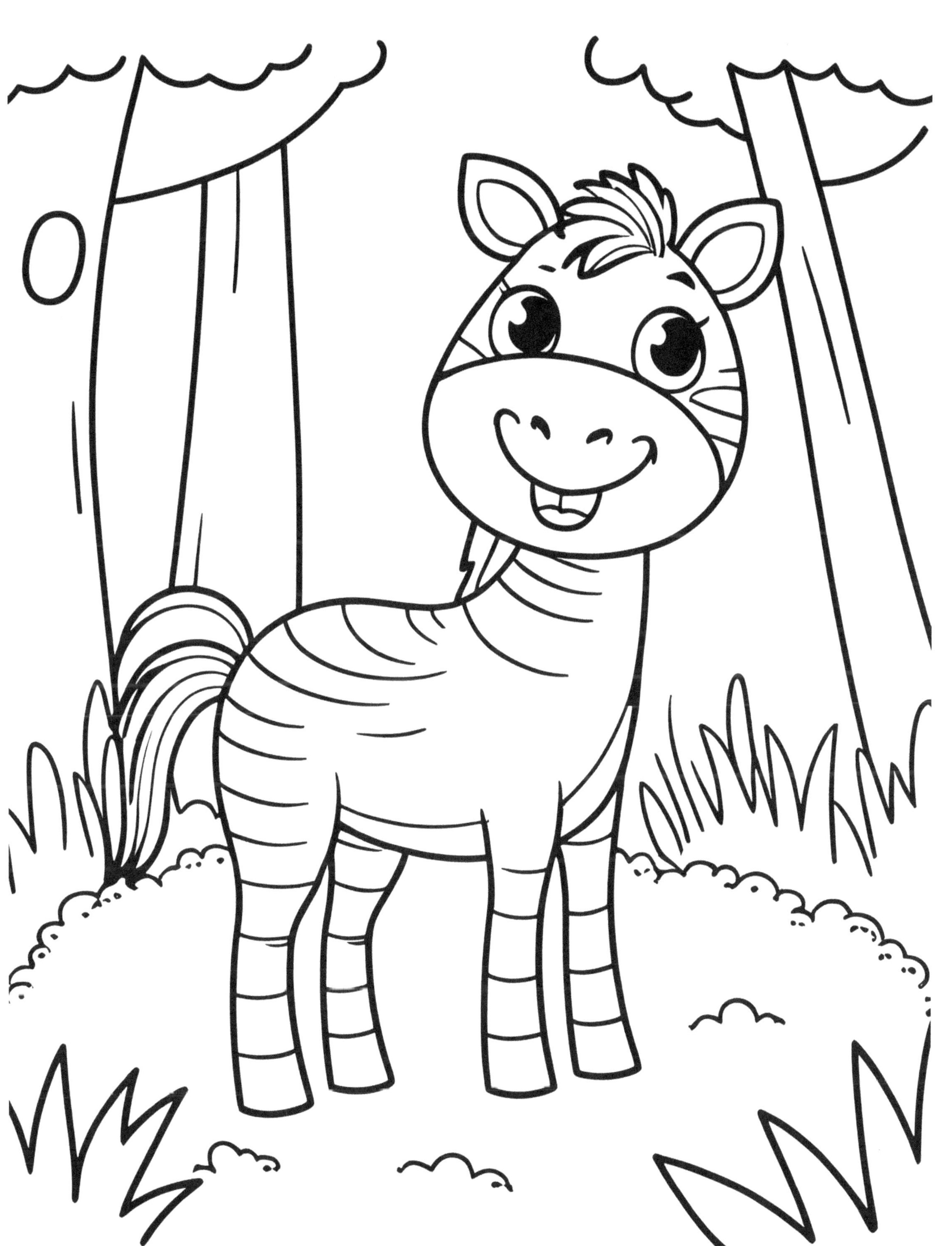

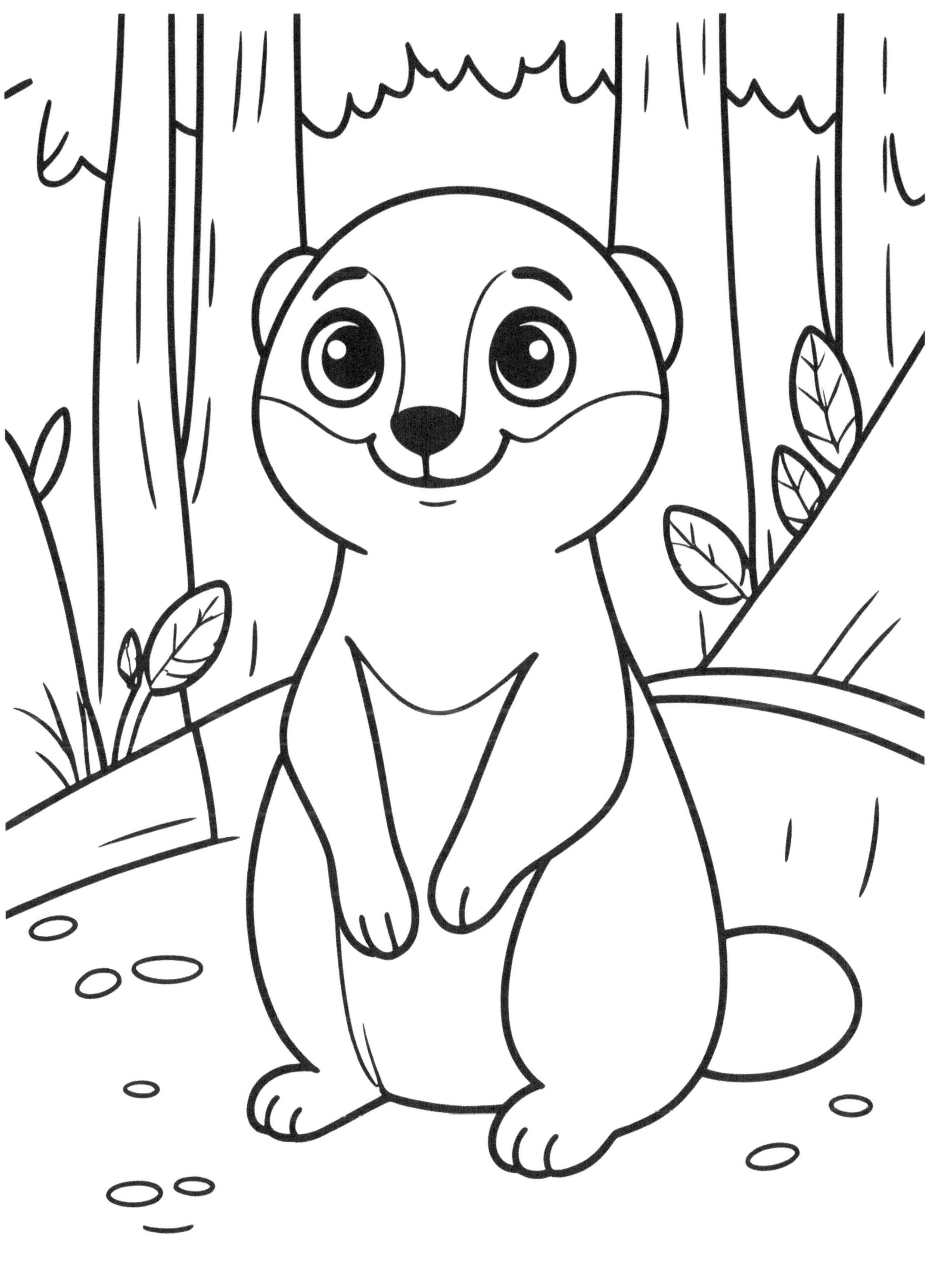

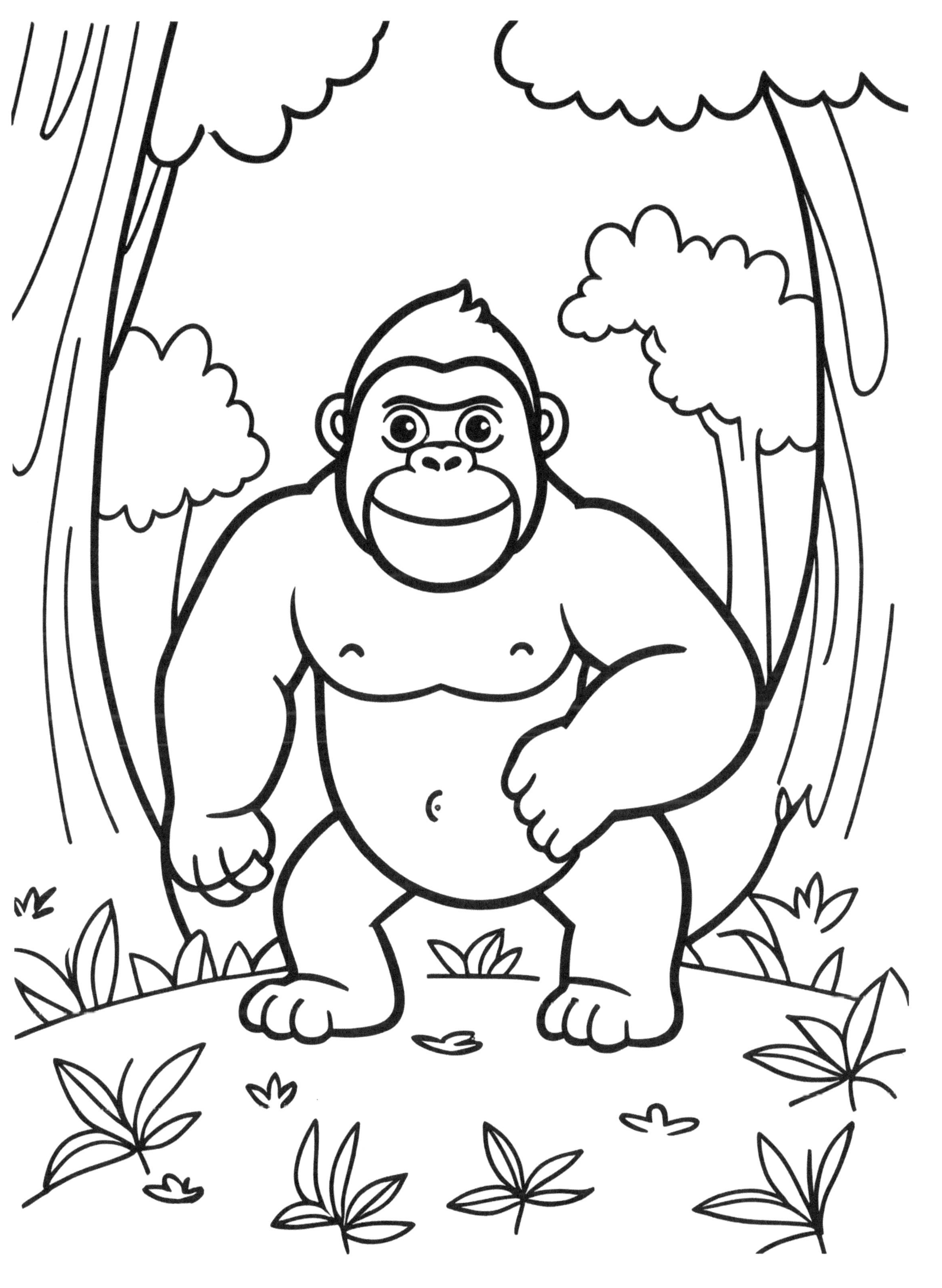

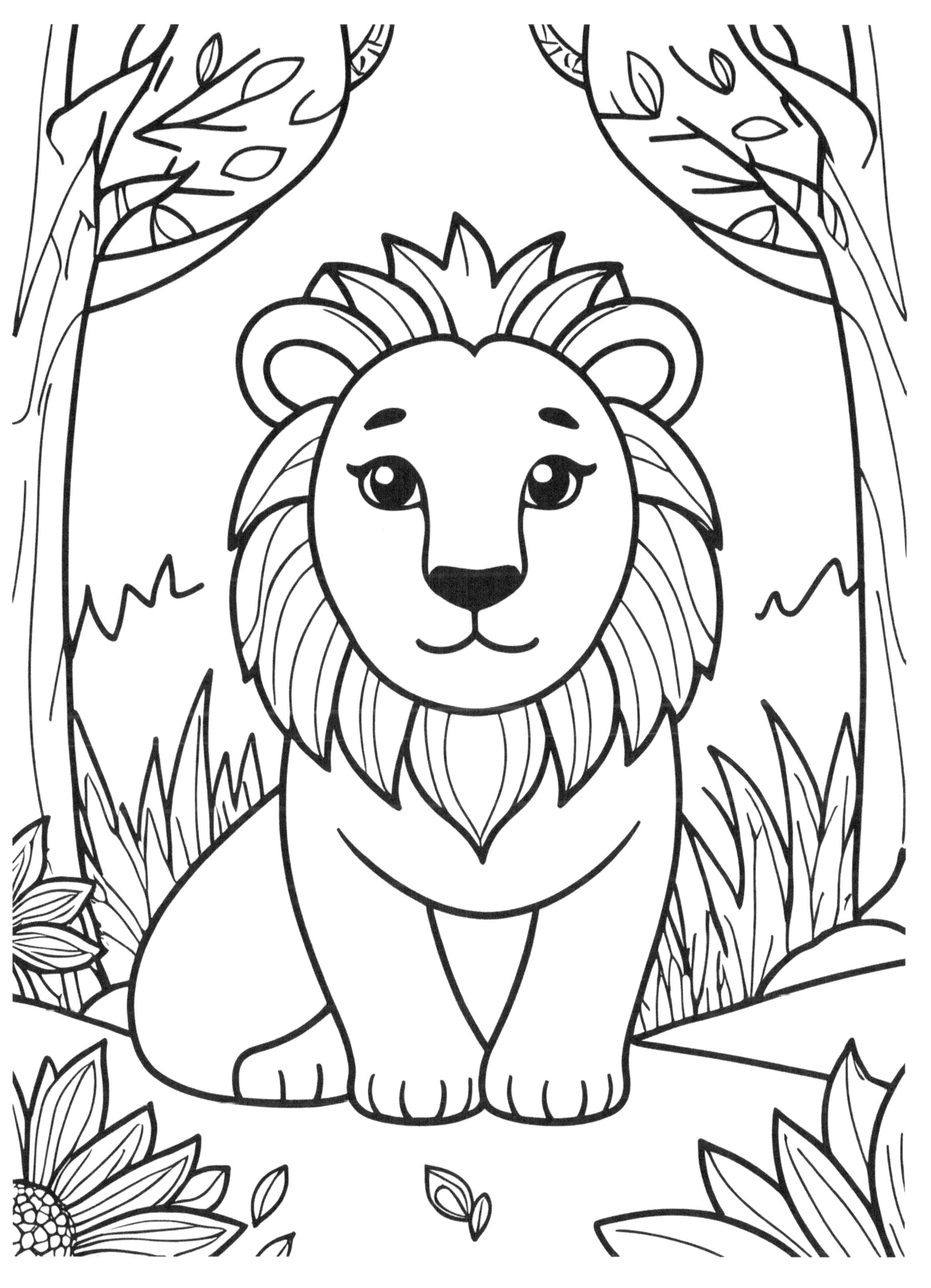

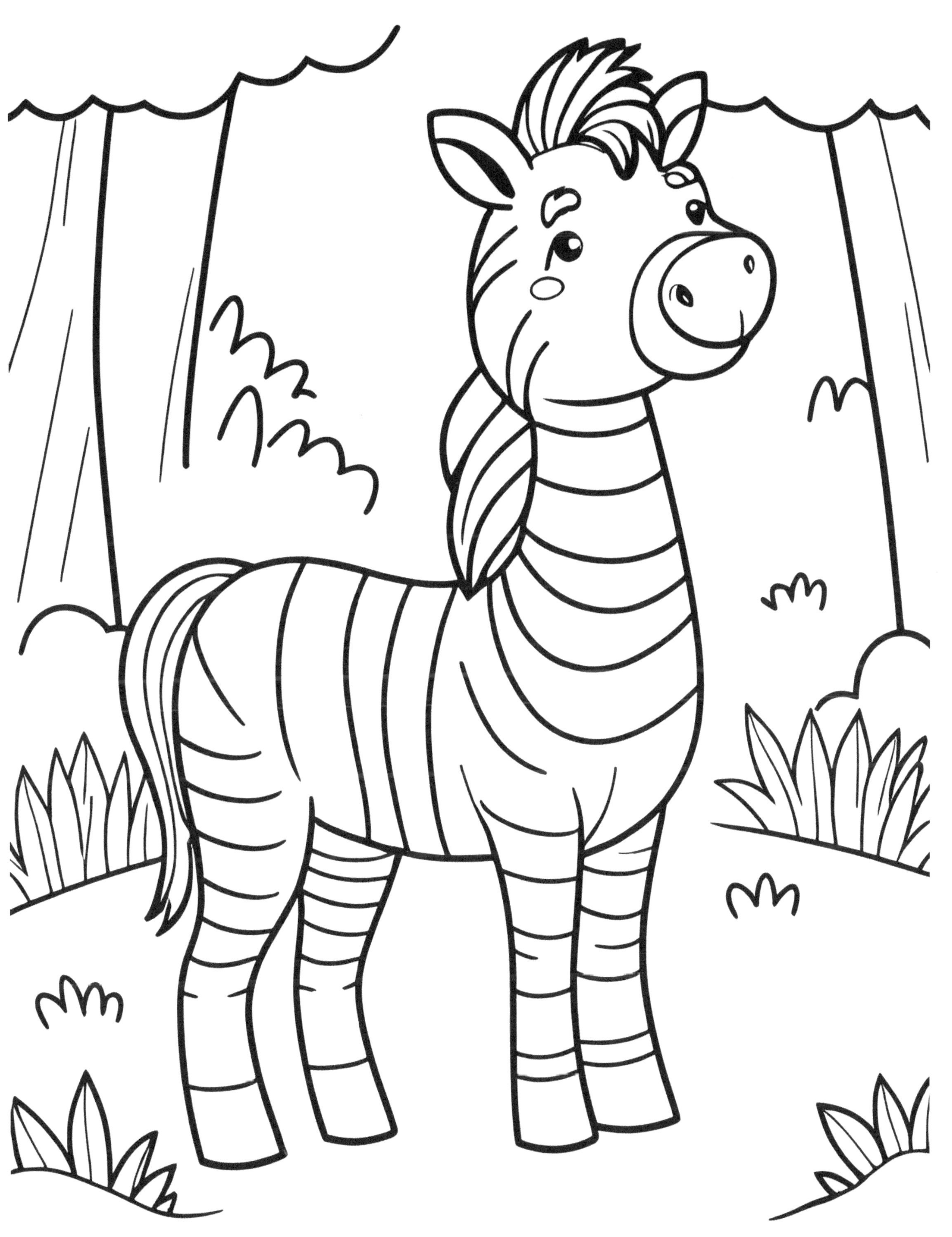

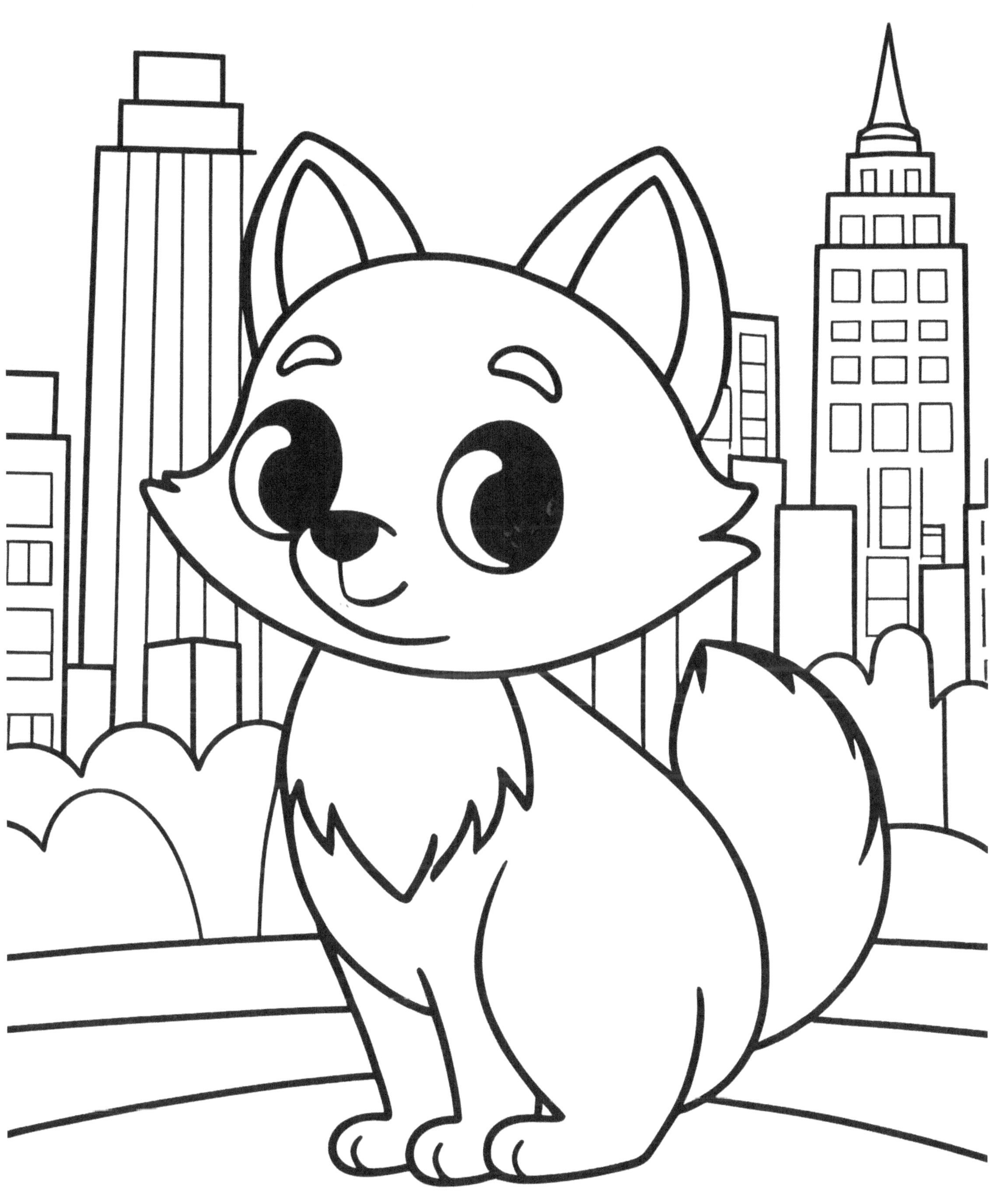

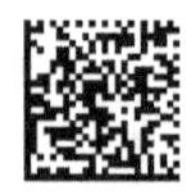

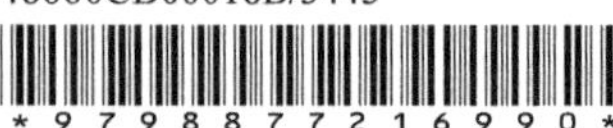
9 798887 216990